THE

Justin –

words w/out arms,
legs, hands.

all my best,

Jim –

FIRST POETS SERIES 3

SERIES EDITOR: ELANA WOLFF

Canada Council for the Arts
Conseil des Arts du Canada

ONTARIO ARTS COUNCIL
CONSEIL DES ARTS DE L'ONTARIO

Guernica Editions Inc. acknowledges the support of
The Canada Council for the Arts.
Guernica Editions Inc. acknowledges the support of
The Ontario Arts Council.

JIM JOHNSTONE

THE VELOCITY OF ESCAPE

GUERNICA

TORONTO – BUFFALO – LANCASTER (U.K.)

2008

Elana Wolff, editor
Guernica Editions Inc.
P.O. Box 117, Station P, Toronto (ON), Canada M5S 2S6
2250 Military Road, Tonawanda, N.Y. 14150-6000 U.S.A.

Distributors:
University of Toronto Press Distribution,
5201 Dufferin Street, Toronto (ON), Canada M3H 5T8
Gazelle Book Services, White Cross Mills, High Town,
Lancaster LA1 4XS U.K.
Independent Publishers Group,
814 N. Franklin Street, Chicago, Il. 60610 U.S.A.

First edition.
Printed in Canada.
Legal Deposit – Fourth Quarter
Library of Congress Catalog Card Number: 2008936845
Library and Archives Canada Cataloguing in Publication
Johnstone, Jim
The velocity of escape / Jim Johnstone.
(First poets series ; 3)
Poems.
ISBN 978-1-55071-292-6
I. Title. II. Series: First poets series (Toronto, Ont.) ; 3
PS8619.O489V44 2008 C811'.6 C2008-905533-0

CONTENTS

for my family
Jim, Gloria, Chris, Iain and Ashley
and for Charles Street

$$V_e = \sqrt{\frac{2GM}{r}}$$

ESCAPE VELOCITY

inside this roll of film
i discover photographs
where i don't exist

moving between thin
grains of light,
towns, cemeteries

although i know
                    (i was there)

this is home,
tall bleached rocks
a white room without doors
or voices

if someone happens to speak
there is no echo
no atmosphere to change
the exposure

or plot an escape
from the gravity
that holds me here.

we kept our reservation at the burning theatre.
outside, it was beginning to snow and you worried
about parking, lipstick marking your teeth.
at the entrance we ripped our own tickets,
blushed with the heavy smoke, the rouge
seats. you insisted on the front row,
loved the way the screen towered like a bonfire
of film stars, not entirely alive. some things
i'll never understand. the way we held hands,
the theatre empty of shine when you began
to undress. i should have expected your claret skin.
i should have been out on the lake, a compass point,
floating small buoys to the beach. the movie glowed
in silence, whatever it was that i wanted to confess.

1

you emerge from eclipse,
a bat over sleeping waters

tongue stuck to black ice,
wet handprints burning, *find me.*

the lake has frozen my footfalls,
your senses; echoes

the lighthouse bouncing
its tired signal in alarm.

a flood of well-wishers disembark
in a rush of high heels,

fishermen swap their catch
for the comfort of a hot meal.

your motel room still won't dry;
an ice bucket overrun with rust,

stained wallpaper that tears
like a streak of chalk.

2

the summer we painted your room blue,
rain began to ransack the forest.

you embraced the deluge like a cutter, licked
the scars that mapped your forearms and wrists

the candy apple shimmer of your apnea,
swelling like blood in the scored veins of the lake.

i dream of your feet rooting on the bottom,
carbon puffs of red discolouring the tide;

your fingers begin to dull and forget your hands,
the hyacinths we scatter on your bed.

it won't be long before you swim
as if water is all you've ever known.

3

we're losing daylight. your breath is
ragged, tubercular, your oar is lead.
it polarizes the tides as if your hands
are magnets, pushes us home. the
shore repeats itself; brothers already
know one another's stories. we both
curse as we lift the nets, empty of all
but mosquitoes, our bony fingers
sifting through.

that never happened. you were gone
by the time we looked for you. the
riverbed stared back with eyes of
limestone, heavy lids. in the afternoon
heat, i managed to propel the canoe on
my own, the tides a vicious watercolour.
peaks of stained glass inclined like a
steeple, pinned my weak strokes to
the shore.

4

by spring, you are reduced
to a hurricane of sand and shells,
an abandoned beach.

i imagine sailing again,
the weight of your body,
the grip of your hand, easily given.

sand spreads like an atlas,
the shore a whisper where i dip
my feet in the undertow.

each time i flinch at the mandible
of a surfacing muskellunge,
your laughter scalds my face.

the dock whines, ties me
to the skeleton of this country,
my bones on your bones.

you huddle, supporting your abdomen,
sort through preserves for dinner;
pickling bottles full of summer tomatoes,
tiny fists submerged with fruit flies and worms,
seeds scattered in the cupboard
waiting to be planted and ripen next year
like the ball of fruit inside of you.

1

the train stutters,
clings to a steel groove in the track;

the glitz of the next town bright
as a match lobbed to boxcar hay.

destination set, the twenty-four hour man
binges on hand-rolled cigarettes

mouths rings of smoke as he explains
the art to a fourteen-year-old runaway –

"paper don't stick wi'out a wad
of spit and tobacco in the husk."

his hands fumble a shirt-pocket zippo,
wrists circled in fine elephant hair.

the train slows in pins of sunlight,
soon the beasts will jolt awake.

the twenty-four hour man clutches his chalk,
prepares to set up an entire world inside a tent.

2

the kiss tastes like a burned
spool of cotton-candy,
the fire-breather's torch
extinguished in a blaze of rapture.

Violet can hear the transformation
of her sister's virgin lips,
the blood dribble from a nick
on the twenty-four hour man's tongue.

she shuts her two-tone eyes,
waits for the gravel warmth
of his palm moving up her thigh,
knows that she and Daisy come together –

Siamese twins share lovers
as certain as accidents happen in threes.

3

railroad ties stretch north,
beginning a noose that
suffocates in malignant coal.

midnight darkens to a compass
point, molts and smothers
on its way to infinity.

southwards, townies thrust
their torches in menace,
sputter with the captive stars.

the twenty-four hour man kicks empty
shotgun shells in boredom,
smears gunpowder on his toes,

wishes he could cough up
ammunition, speak backwards
until the hours begin again.

adenine

failures unravel,
mutate and flood
the empty riverbeds
of your skin.
a cool stream
of reptilian blood
calms the itch
of fresh scales,
brightens as links
in your code
appear.

guanine

chromosomes
split like treble
and bass coaxed
from a jukebox –
i take your lead
and we begin
to waltz
in three-quarter time,
a template
where the sweetest
melodies repeat.

cytosine

it doesn't matter
if you stay up
the entire night
peeling limes,
your guests have
already stuffed
themselves
with good bacteria,
know that all
your recipes
are set.

thymine

a nightly
attraction,
you digest
razor blades
and wipe your
wrists clean
of scar tissue,
insist this
is the only way
to keep us
together.

pouring carefully,
she drops an
extra spoon into her tea

twins

milk and sugar
clouding the future.

she lets the mixture
warm her belly,
bloom and pull apart –

uterus like a teacup
face down

gravity lured
to the rim without
separating the stalks.

in his stride, the wire-walker is already tragic. he bends to tighten his peacock shoes, whistles *unforget-table* through the dressing room. past red velvet, his breath is gulped by the audience, applause thunders for the aerialists. they're returning home, were born to the vocabulary of balance. they mount, footholds unbotched until the wire-walker mistakes gyrations of cable for concrete. stop for step. the pyramid disintegrates as quickly as it formed, a rain of limp bodies plummeting like loose grains of sand in an hourglass. breaking from the bleachers, the crowd suspends their belief with broken skulls and blood smeared on faulty rigging.

they twist their wrists together,
reach for the telephone

fibre optic cables
insulated in musculature.

dialtone snakes out
like a pulse, squeezes
through thin black wires

blood pooling
in the plastic receiver
of two hearts.

circulation mixes with current,
doubles at the point
of intersection

        the flesh of a wrist
        picking
                        up.

THE TRAPEZE ARTIST

1

orange balls and lit torches
blur like a swarm of flies

defy the atmosphere
so that only a juggler
can recognize their beauty

tumbling towards the ground
in slow motion like setting suns.

2

before each performance
the bearded woman
extends her hands to my face,

slides them down
my rouged cheeks,
the bare surface of elephant tusks.

despite our matching breasts
and the presence of the alligator man,
we all have different reasons
for being here.

3

swinging against gravity
on the trapeze

my stomach drops
the length of my body
and my feet are useless,

broken wings tucking into me,
obsessing over the ground.

4

vanishing is my magnum opus,
standing in clouds
of aluminium powder,

losing and reattaching bodies

before returning to the stage
for a curtain call.

the hospital beds
are covered in layered
green sheets,

pressed together as if
pressure alone
can merge fabric.

the twins dream
of wearing watches
to cover scars,

telling time beneath
artificial light and curtains
that divide the room;

separating the dead
from the next miracle

while surgeons fit
their masks
and slice into bone.

THESE PEOPLE ARE DANGEROUS

1

acrobats mount in a triangle,
arms exacting themselves
on the marquee,
a heartbeat of living canvas.

the multitudes push
inwards

talking of spectacle
and four-fingered jugglers,
but praying for death –

the kind of massacre
children remember
in glorious photographs
or silent movies.

2

a contortionist moves
like the lips of two men kissing,

serpentine tongues
unafraid of
God.

3

tents collapse,
rainwater washes identities,
blood, semen,
red cranberries trampled and crushed.

performers illuminate
the night's shadows –
fireflies leaping
in an overturned glass.

FIREWORKS

i want splendor
and exploding crystals
to become my skin,
another beginning,
every sense
a live wire.

in the distance
small pops
and a quiet rain of colours,
the spectrum of an anarchist
before the hush and smoke
of death.

tonight the magicians
have the most beautiful
shirt sleeves.

QUARANTINE

viruses divide,
travel down separate throats;

the beginnings of strep
exploding like bottle rockets
in siamese veins.

mother weeps in the corner
while doctors wheeze
through their masks;

silk scarves curl out
from between the twins' lips,

white blood cells
rushing to contaminate
the room from a single breath,

airborne and rising.

APOLLO 14

details crowd us, a fistful of matches,
cardboard glittering with heat
and slick amphetamines.

the cool perfume of teenage girls
replaces morning's sulphur,
devolves with speed that fizzles
under our anxious tongues.

we enter the local convenience store,
begin to stuff our bloodless pockets
with wax lips and gobstoppers.

John leans over the lotto counter,
pays for his coke with half a two dollar bill,
while astronauts scatter like ghosts
on the surface of the moon.

deserted, Alan Shepard cracks the shuttle's seal,
inhales a shooting fever,
knee deep in craters of scrap metal.

he walks above us, a common thief
restlessly sifting barren earth.

we try our luck at a game of pinball,
fire silver planets into the sky.

DIALTONE

they wake up with blood
on their wrists,
                                        waves
barely audible in their veins.

touching separate wounds
a receiver lifts to their ears,
empty hum
                                        reverberating.

with connections severed
and no one to call
they hang up,

their lives moving apart
as if one or the other
dialled the wrong number.

PHANTOM LIMBS

the needle plunges down,
sleep crawls into his arm
with beads of anaesthetic.

his body is weighted
to cement blocks,
bound and shoved
                                        overboard,
settles calmly
with charred leaves
and silt in the waves.

waking to move
phantom limbs,
the tide leaks from his mouth,

pours to his amputated
hand

flicking on lights
like burnt nerves
even though he is alone.

at a family picnic the twins halve
slices of watermelon
and spit velvet seeds
across the lawn,

stretch as far away from one
another as they can;

heaving water balloons
back and forth until all
their relatives are wet
where the rubber breaks.

THREE-LEGGED

after the gunshot,
uncles and cousins
hesitate at the starting line,
bend uncomfortably
in grass-stained
burlap sacs.

the twins touch
in more than one place,
their legs bound
by unnecessary ropes,
incised flesh
forcing them to limp.

BAITING HOOKS

baiting hooks,
the twins flick the heads
of wriggling minnows,

silver scales flail the air,
attracting blackflies.

blood is up for grabs
in the summer heat,

wind mixes with yellow fire,
howls over the lip
of father's Corona.

he stuffs a lime down the neck
to adjust the pitch,
traps his thumb.

laughter shakes the twins'
warm bodies closer;

they drop their hooks
for anything that will bite.

HULAPOPPERS

cast out beyond the bulrushes
my naked hook swims
in Scugog's shallow warmth,
scrapes the bottom, all silver teeth
and calculated menace.

horseflies continue their whine
as the boat sputters to silence,
drifts aimlessly to the highway
for a look at the rainbow of freshly abandoned lures
dancing on the powerlines.

rusted jitterbugs and the frayed
skirts of hulapoppers
catch in the lips of fishermen,
graphite rods starve for the gleam of minnows,
the gentle struggle of bait.

barbs set in my jawline
pull me across the miles of water
i have left to travel,
crude gasoline searing my lungs
like an amphora bonfire.

i propel home with the rattle
of a dirty bucket for muskellunge heads,
a dull knife to sever line;
minus a strike, my net
is an empty necessity.

SWEET'N'LOW

from habit
he takes two cups
out of the cupboard,

pours coffee into milk
with his right hand.

he doesn't need to ask
"one lump or two,"

already knows
that his twin
takes sweet'n'low

and even though he is
walking through
a different house
smoking cigarettes

he is wearing
the same clothes.

lightning fragments the twins' senses,
brushes past their cheeks
like a gypsy moth.

their irises flush blue,
colour sucked
into orbit, off-kilter

recalling the day they ate
ice-cream from the same cone,
three scoops
of mint chocolate-chip –

sugar spiked their blood,
surfaced on blistered skin,
a burning filament
hemorrhaging electricity,

forking the distance
on two heavy wings.

BODY DOUBLES

our faces are mirrors
convex and misshapen
where they touch
in vague spokes
two ships reaching out
to a lighthouse
you offer me
a bouquet of wires
throw electricity
as our guests
sip gin in seats
designated
bride and groom
even though
we met each one
of them together

this typeface
will never escape
its scales and skin
the words that exist
without arms legs hands
like a snake
read aloud they
fork your tongue
and transform the hiss
of the sea we share
into separate desires
side by side
Renoir's lovers
in The Swing
who stand together
but never meet

A RELIABLE CURE

vein open, you flip pages
of dirty history –

your tongue beating
foreign lips,

the prick of a cat's saliva
in your forearm.

carefully, you boil cells,
wipe the cold trail

of mucus from your skin,
the salted leech

that digests chapters
of your blood.

in time, your heart twitches
with fresh pain,

a puncture; hemorrhages
rough ink.

at last, proof that you
live here.

BLOODLETTING

the bloat of poison, lancet
and leech, your bruises
understand the journey,

have travelled beneath
your skin like an unlovely
river, baby blue mascara
on closed eyes.

you called me Jesse James,
put your fist through
a jukebox the day we met,

wanted a witness to suffer
your release, peel newsprint
in torpid strips to stop the leaves
rivering from your veins.

you had your father's hands,
never bled in denim
or tumbleweed;

fingers trained to splay locks,
ribbon and collapse
in the clockwork of a steel heart,
the buttonhooks of my chest.

headlights fan out, tentacles
submerged in the darkness,
your '83 Buick lighting up
the tracks behind the bingo hall.
the two of us kick up sand,
assemble split wood into a bonfire
of overgrown grass and the shimmering
orange veins of railroad ties.
the blaze of our Du Mauriers climbs
with embers of car exhaust,
voices thick with whisky,
surging into a cacophony of laughter
and smoldering fire. when it quiets
we hear the pop and sizzle of grasshoppers
in the disarray of the inferno,
the snap of your ankle,
bone releasing along a break,
you collapsing to the sober ground.

IMMUNE RESPONSE

nothing intrudes on your fall,
artificial night, the water in a snow globe,
your sermon a chorus of rubber soles,
cracked pavement.

immune to the glare of streetlamps,
i've seen you defy the sidewalk's pull
on stilts, dissolve from sight
like sugar cubes in a stiff drink.

tonight the highway is soundless,
a vacuum of exhaust and sleep,
my eyes weighted, hooked down
with the comfort of motion.

i relax, knowing you could lift the car
if we needed to get out of here,
shift my attention away
from the warning strip and its alarm.

you respond quickly, shift the wheel
to the left, antibodies sprinting
through your circulation – fire
steering us into the unknown.

submerged headfirst in the silver
of water and glass,
the tides flood my straitjacket,
beat my chest in surges
like the hands of a concert pianist.

spectators gather at the tank's partition,
listen for the rattle of keys,
the ring of individual fingers
that will be tested
in the question mark of a wall socket.

a blur of meat and electricity,
my bindings are a diversion
from the procession of arthritic locks,
the corrosion of my pale breath
before the split-second escape;

the precise struggle of my torso
when i cast off my manacles,
a metallic snakeskin,
my chest airtight and gleaming
with a bright row of steel keys.

filaments pop and flicker
vacancy, the red alphabet
of prom queens and used car
salesmen printed behind
motel doors.

checking in with dusk,
comets eavesdrop
against the bulge of my flesh,
atoms split and drag
their oily tails in lead.

next to the ice dispenser,
room 305 gapes open,
a revolved tube of lipstick
stuck to the nightstand
like a candy-apple.

i abandon my filthy bucket,
pocket the Gideon,
and pray that the Coke
machine's spark will light
my trail to the pool.

in sweaty chlorine i drown
stars and dead leaves,
steer dark continents
through the wrong end
of my binoculars.

my sister died of the
most wonderful cancer,

a malignancy that hung
in miniature on her eyelashes
and brought heavy sleep in the night.

it wasn't the type of cancer
that spread through hands;

when i held her
she was warm to the touch,

a heat that stretched
through her heart and lungs until
she held flames

so bright i no longer
saw her body

or how the tumour became
photosynthetic,
a blindspot in her leaves.

this afternoon's cadaver can't shrink away
from the approach of my blade,
destiny clearly outlined in black marker,

an instruction to *cut here*, scissors rifling
the pages of *Vanity Fair*
for a collage of heads, neckties and shoulders.

flesh yields to my first incision like wet sand,
identity receding from your throat
in a tide of cracked bone,

crumpled paper glued above vocal chords,
the beginnings of collapse
in a soundproof room.

there's something fierce in your preservation,
the burn of crude formaldehyde
on inadequate skin, the story you tell

when opened up: there were cigarettes after sex,
nights you refused to kiss
saying "i want to leave" again and again.

the radio broadcasts our orbit,
drones in bands of static
and useless aluminum,
lonely frequencies enticing
listeners at the other end
of tongue or telescope.

no closer to the ragged
wiring of the stars,
dark bodies decompress,
pixilate in negative space
while astronauts drift
in layers of white rubber.

nothing is shared, recycled air,
panic, x/y chromosomes
passed in a handshake
sterile as the cosmos itself,
wireless and closing around
a shuttle of weightless fire.

anchored to new cisterns
the astronauts hold their breaths,
wait for stars to implode,
heat the algorithms
they can see more clearly
in the sky's imbalance.

BURN

when your cardboard apartment
caught fire, you lit up –
the heat bearing flat scars
along your shoulders and stomach.

Nancy Sinatra filled the stereo,
a hand-rolled cigarette dropped
its tip, a bouncing sun on the carpet,
igniting your scarlet hair
with the consistency of melting glass.

we spent afternoons in the heat,
transforming our skin into something harder,
something wild and dangerous

until you lost control of voluntary reactions,
mouth open like Janet Leigh in a bathtub,
hands on your face peeling away in blazing strips
to reveal primal elements
you had never thought to share;

vanity like white bandages,
covering the smooth reminders of how you burned.

METHODS OF SURVIVAL

1

no snapshots should be taken

while the deer
pose at their saltlicks.

2

despite the mosquito lamps
that hang in abandoned tents
you can expect to lose a little blood,
dreams slipping through circles
the size of a child's hand.

clench your fist over flame
and watch it grow the hair of beasts
as the night animals vanish
and fuse with your body

a totem
each shape alive in you.

3

if you are confronted
with any wild animals

keep repeating

"i am a tree in this forest"
until you disappear.

ACKNOWLEDGEMENTS

Some of the poems in this manuscript have previously appeared in *Acta Victoriana, Canadian Literature, Carousel, Contemporary Verse 2, dANDelion, Descant, dig, existere, Grain, Grimm Magazine, The Hart House Review, Lantern, The Malahat Review, Matrix, The Naskwaak Review, Route 2* and the chapbook *siamese poems* (Surly Editions, 2006).

"quarantine," "conjoined dreams," "phantom limbs," and "lichtenberg figures" were awarded the 2005-2006 E. J. Pratt Medal and Prize in Poetry.

Special thanks to: Vicki Sloot – for her friendship and support. Ian Williams – my first reader, for the misunderstandings. Elana Wolff and Antonio D'Alfonso – for their invaluable insight and faith in my work. Also – Phlip Arima, Clara Blackwood, Alex Boyd, Veronika Bryskiewicz, Rachael Cogar, Heather Cohrs, Kristin Connor, "Surly" Dani Couture, Stacey-May Fowles, Devon Gallant, Luigi Gentile, Julie Cameron Gray, Jim and Audrey Johnstone, Mark Laliberte, Don McKay, Leigh Nash, Sandy Pool, Frank and Helen Treml and Myna Wallin.

transcontinental

Printed on Rolland Enviro 100, containing 100% post-consumer recycled fibers, Eco-Logo certified, Proceded without chlorinate, FSC Recycled and manufactured using biogaz energy.